THE JOHN MERRILL WALK RECORD BOOK

BY

JOHN N. MERRILL

PHOTOGRAPHS BY JOHN N. MERRILL

a J.N.M. PUBLICATION

1986

a J.N.M. PUBLICATION

Conceived, edited, typset and designed by John N. Merrill.

© Copyright—text and design—John N. Merrill 1986

© Copyright— photographs—John N. Merrill 1986

First Published November 1986

ISBN 0 907496 47 4

J.N.M. Publications, Winster, Matlock, Derbyshire. DE4 2DQ

Typesetting interfaced by:
Steve Rothwell Typesetting Services, 20 St Ann's Square, Manchester.

Printed by: Adams & Sons (Printers) Ltd., Blueschool Street, Hereford.

CONTENTS

NAMCHE BAZAR

REMEMBER AND OBSERVE
THE COUNTRY CODE

ENJOY THE COUNTRYSIDE AND RESPECT ITS LIFE AND WORK.

GUARD AGAINST ALL RISK OF FIRE.

FASTEN ALL GATES.

KEEP YOUR DOGS UNDER CLOSE CONTROL.

KEEP TO PUBLIC PATHS ACROSS FARMLAND.

USE GATES AND STILES TO CROSS FENCES, HEDGES AND WALLS.

LEAVE LIVESTOCK, CROPS AND MACHINERY ALONE.

TAKE YOUR LITTER HOME—PACK IT IN, PACK IT OUT.

HELP TO KEEP ALL WATER CLEAN.

PROTECT WILDLIFE, PLANTS AND TREES.

TAKE SPECIAL CARE ON COUNTRY ROADS.

MAKE NO UNNECESSARY NOISE.

PEMBROKESHIRE COAST

ABOUT JOHN N. MERRILL

John combines the characteristics and strength of a mountain climber with the stamina, and athletic capabilities of a marathon runner. In this respect he is unique and has to his credit a whole string of remarkable long walks. He is without question the world's leading marathon walker.

Over the last ten years he has walked more than 55,000 miles and successfully completed ten walks of at least 1,000 miles or more.

His six walks in Britain are—

Hebridean Journey ....1,003 miles
Northern Isles Journey ....913 miles
Irish Island Journey...1,578 miles
Parkland Journey ....2,043 miles
Lands End to John O'Groats...................................1,608 miles

and in 1978 he became the first person (permanent Guinness Book Of Records entry) to walk the entire coastline of Britain—6,824 miles in ten months.

In Europe he has walked across Austria (712 miles), hiked the Tour of Mont Blanc and GR20 in Corsica as training! In 1982 he walked across Europe—2,806 miles in 107 days—crossing seven countries, the Swiss and French Alps and the complete Pyrennean chain—the hardest and longest mountain walk in Europe.

In America he used the world's longest footpath—The Appalachian Trail (2,200 miles) as a training walk. The following year he walked from Mexico to Canada in record time—118 days for 2,700 miles.

During the summer of 1984, John set off from Virginia Beach on the Atlantic coast, and walked 4,226 miles without a rest day, across the width of America to San Francisco and the Pacific Ocean. This walk is unquestionably his greatest achievement, being, in modern history, the longest, hardest crossing of the USA in the shortest time—under six months (177 days). The direct distance is 2,800 miles.

Between major walks John is out training in his own area —the Peak District National Park. As well as walking in other areas of Britain and in Europe he has been trekking in the Himalayas four times. He lectures extensively and is author of more than sixty books.

1

WALKING IN THE PEAK DISTRICT—CHATSWORTH PARK

INTRODUCTION

The last few years have seen me walking in different parts of the world. In the space of a month, just recently, I was doing day walks in the Peak District National Park, following tow paths in Staffordshire and Cheshire, and walking a couple of High Level routes in the Italian Dolomites. At the end of each walk I felt frustrated at not being able to record the day's outing for future reference—hence this book!

Instead of writing comments and recording my walk in the guide I was using, I felt there was a need for a book to simply allow one to record one's walk, be it a day or a longer one. My aim of this book is to rectify this, allowing a page per walk to record the walk undertaken, what maps and guides used, what area, comments on it and what the weather did, the pub at lunchtime and what flowers and birds seen etc. There is, I hope, ample room to record a year's walking and space to include details of challenge or longer walks undertaken.

In time I shall have a yearly display of record books and in my twilight years can browse through them and recall the days on a Lakeland fell, or a stroll by the sea or trekking in the Andes. I hope you find the record book of use—and pleasant walking!

Happy walking!

JOHN N. MERRILL

WALK NO: 3	DATE: August 8th 1986

COUNTY/AREA:	LAKE DISTRICT

MAPS USED:	1:25,000 O.S. - N.W. sheet

GUIDE BOOKS:	J. MERRILL'S - "LAKELAND TOPS"

START POINT: WASTWATER	DISTANCE: 16 MILES

ROUTE OUTLINE: WASTWATER - PAVEY ARK - RED PIKE - GREAT GABLE - WASTWATER

WEATHER: Hot & sunny - perfect day of good clarity

COMMENTS: Logged walk through some of England's finest scenery, high fells with superb views of Ennerdale valley and Sellafield! Few people about and good to enjoy the solitude. The ascent of Gable a bit hard on George who complained of blisters in his new boots! Great scree run down - good to get the legs working - 10 min top to bottom; must be getting fit!

PUB: Napes Needle: pate and claret for a change!

BIRDS: Skylark, Red Grouse, Fieldfare, Sparrowhawk.	FLOWERS: Bog asphodil, Mountain Pansy, heath orchid.

3

DAY WALK RECORD

WALK NO:	DATE: 27TH DEC 1992

COUNTY/AREA: SOUTHWELL

MAPS USED: O.S. LANDRANGER 120

GUIDE BOOKS:

START POINT: EASTHORPE	DISTANCE: APPROX 8 MILES

ROUTE OUTLINE: EASTHORPE - SOUTHWELL RACE CSE - ROLLESTON - UPTON - EASTHORPE

WEATHER: OVERCASTE BUT DRY

COMMENTS: GOOD WALKING, BUT WET UNDER FOOT. GOING STICKY IN PLACES. AREA NEW TO EVERYONE BUT A GOOD TIME HAD BY ALL. RATHER FLAT LAND, WE HAD FUN WITH A HORSE IN A FIELD BY UPTON MILL A GOOD LUNCH ENJOYED IN THE CROWN INN PRECEEDED BY A WARM WELCOME. A GOOD WALK FOR A FIRST OFFERING BUT WILL MY REPUTATION PROCEED ME?

PUB: CROWN INN, ROLLESTON

BIRDS:	FLOWERS:

4

WALK NO:	DATE: 22-1-95

COUNTY/AREA: BELPER DUFFIELD

MAPS USED:

GUIDE BOOKS:

START POINT: EAST MILL BELPER	DISTANCE: APPROX 9-10 MILES

ROUTE OUTLINE: EAST MILL - DERWENT - DUFFIELD - WINDLEY - HAZELWOOD - CHEVIN BANK - BELPER

WEATHER: COOL BUT DRY. BECOMING OVERCAST

COMMENTS: WET AND MUDDY UNDERFOOT, CERTAIN STILES UNPASSABLE DUE TO WATER. NEW GROUND TO ALL AND VERY ENJOYABLE COMPANY. PLENTY OF COUNTRYSIDE VIEWS AND REASONABLE WEATHER. LUNCH ENJOYED BY EVERYONE AFTER BEING TURNED AWAY FROM NEW INN (SILLY MAN!). A MUST FOR A REVISIT DURING DRYER WEATHER. JB.

PUB: PATTERN MAKERS ARMS - DUFFIELD

~~BIRDS.~~ FOX (PYE BRIDGE) SQUIRRELS (GREY x4) RABBIT.	FLOWERS:

WALK NO:	DATE:
COUNTY/AREA:	
MAPS USED:	
GUIDE BOOKS:	
START POINT:	DISTANCE:
ROUTE OUTLINE:	
WEATHER:	
COMMENTS:	
PUB:	
BIRDS:	FLOWERS:

WALK NO:	DATE:
COUNTY/AREA:	
MAPS USED:	
GUIDE BOOKS:	
START POINT:	DISTANCE:
ROUTE OUTLINE:	
WEATHER:	
COMMENTS:	
PUB:	
BIRDS:	FLOWERS:

WALK NO:	DATE:

COUNTY/AREA:

MAPS USED:

GUIDE BOOKS:

START POINT:	DISTANCE:

ROUTE OUTLINE:

WEATHER:

COMMENTS:

PUB:

BIRDS:	FLOWERS:

WALK NO:	DATE:

COUNTY/AREA:

MAPS USED:

GUIDE BOOKS:

START POINT:	DISTANCE:

ROUTE OUTLINE:

WEATHER:

COMMENTS:

PUB:

BIRDS:	FLOWERS:

WALK NO:	DATE:
COUNTY/AREA:	
MAPS USED:	
GUIDE BOOKS:	
START POINT:	DISTANCE:
ROUTE OUTLINE:	
WEATHER:	
COMMENTS:	
PUB:	
BIRDS:	FLOWERS:

WALK NO:	DATE:
COUNTY/AREA:	
MAPS USED:	
GUIDE BOOKS:	
START POINT:	DISTANCE:
ROUTE OUTLINE:	
WEATHER:	
COMMENTS:	
PUB:	
BIRDS:	FLOWERS:

WALK NO:	DATE:
COUNTY/AREA:	
MAPS USED:	
GUIDE BOOKS:	
START POINT:	DISTANCE:
ROUTE OUTLINE:	
WEATHER:	
COMMENTS:	
PUB:	
BIRDS:	FLOWERS:

WALK NO:	DATE:
COUNTY/AREA:	
MAPS USED:	
GUIDE BOOKS:	
START POINT:	DISTANCE:
ROUTE OUTLINE:	
WEATHER:	
COMMENTS:	
PUB:	
BIRDS:	FLOWERS:

WALK NO:	DATE:
COUNTY/AREA:	
MAPS USED:	
GUIDE BOOKS:	
START POINT:	DISTANCE:
ROUTE OUTLINE:	
WEATHER:	
COMMENTS:	
PUB:	
BIRDS:	FLOWERS:

WALK NO:	DATE:
COUNTY/AREA:	
MAPS USED:	
GUIDE BOOKS:	
START POINT:	DISTANCE:
ROUTE OUTLINE:	
WEATHER:	
COMMENTS:	
PUB:	
BIRDS:	FLOWERS:

WALK NO:	DATE:
COUNTY/AREA:	
MAPS USED:	
GUIDE BOOKS:	
START POINT:	DISTANCE:
ROUTE OUTLINE:	
WEATHER:	
COMMENTS:	
PUB:	
BIRDS:	FLOWERS:

WALK NO:	DATE:
COUNTY/AREA:	
MAPS USED:	
GUIDE BOOKS:	
START POINT:	DISTANCE:
ROUTE OUTLINE:	
WEATHER:	
COMMENTS:	
PUB:	
BIRDS:	FLOWERS:

WALK NO:	DATE:
COUNTY/AREA:	
MAPS USED:	
GUIDE BOOKS:	
START POINT:	DISTANCE:
ROUTE OUTLINE:	
WEATHER:	
COMMENTS:	
PUB:	
BIRDS:	FLOWERS:

WALK NO:	DATE:
COUNTY/AREA:	
MAPS USED:	
GUIDE BOOKS:	
START POINT:	DISTANCE:
ROUTE OUTLINE:	
WEATHER:	
COMMENTS:	
PUB:	
BIRDS:	FLOWERS:

WALK NO:	DATE:
COUNTY/AREA:	
MAPS USED:	
GUIDE BOOKS:	
START POINT:	DISTANCE:
ROUTE OUTLINE:	
WEATHER:	
COMMENTS:	
PUB:	
BIRDS:	FLOWERS:

WALK NO:	DATE:
COUNTY/AREA:	
MAPS USED:	
GUIDE BOOKS:	
START POINT:	DISTANCE:
ROUTE OUTLINE:	
WEATHER:	
COMMENTS:	
PUB:	
BIRDS:	FLOWERS:

WALK NO:	DATE:
COUNTY/AREA:	
MAPS USED:	
GUIDE BOOKS:	
START POINT:	DISTANCE:
ROUTE OUTLINE:	
WEATHER:	
COMMENTS:	
PUB:	
BIRDS:	FLOWERS:

WALK NO:	DATE:
COUNTY/AREA:	
MAPS USED:	
GUIDE BOOKS:	
START POINT:	DISTANCE:
ROUTE OUTLINE:	
WEATHER:	
COMMENTS:	
PUB:	
BIRDS:	FLOWERS:

WALK NO:	DATE:
COUNTY/AREA:	
MAPS USED:	
GUIDE BOOKS:	
START POINT:	DISTANCE:
ROUTE OUTLINE:	
WEATHER:	
COMMENTS:	

PUB:	
BIRDS:	FLOWERS:

WALK NO:	DATE:
COUNTY/AREA:	
MAPS USED:	
GUIDE BOOKS:	
START POINT:	DISTANCE:
ROUTE OUTLINE:	
WEATHER:	
COMMENTS:	
PUB:	
BIRDS:	FLOWERS:

WALK NO:	DATE:
COUNTY/AREA:	
MAPS USED:	
GUIDE BOOKS:	
START POINT:	DISTANCE:
ROUTE OUTLINE:	
WEATHER:	
COMMENTS:	
PUB:	
BIRDS:	FLOWERS:

WALK NO:	DATE:
COUNTY/AREA:	
MAPS USED:	
GUIDE BOOKS:	
START POINT:	DISTANCE:
ROUTE OUTLINE:	
WEATHER:	
COMMENTS:	

PUB:

BIRDS:	FLOWERS:

WALK NO:	DATE:
COUNTY/AREA:	
MAPS USED:	
GUIDE BOOKS:	
START POINT:	DISTANCE:
ROUTE OUTLINE:	
WEATHER:	
COMMENTS:	
PUB:	
BIRDS:	FLOWERS:

WALK NO:	DATE:
COUNTY/AREA:	
MAPS USED:	
GUIDE BOOKS:	
START POINT:	DISTANCE:
ROUTE OUTLINE:	
WEATHER:	
COMMENTS:	
PUB:	
BIRDS:	FLOWERS:

WALK NO:	DATE:

COUNTY/AREA:

MAPS USED:

GUIDE BOOKS:

START POINT:	DISTANCE:

ROUTE OUTLINE:

WEATHER:

COMMENTS:

PUB:

BIRDS:	FLOWERS:

WALK NO:	DATE:

COUNTY/AREA:

MAPS USED:

GUIDE BOOKS:

START POINT:	DISTANCE:

ROUTE OUTLINE:

WEATHER:

COMMENTS:

PUB:

BIRDS:	FLOWERS:

WALK NO:	DATE:
COUNTY/AREA:	
MAPS USED:	
GUIDE BOOKS:	
START POINT:	DISTANCE:
ROUTE OUTLINE:	
WEATHER:	
COMMENTS:	
PUB:	
BIRDS:	FLOWERS:

WALK NO:	DATE:
COUNTY/AREA:	
MAPS USED:	
GUIDE BOOKS:	
START POINT:	DISTANCE:
ROUTE OUTLINE:	
WEATHER:	
COMMENTS:	
PUB:	
BIRDS:	FLOWERS:

WALK NO:	DATE:
COUNTY/AREA:	
MAPS USED:	
GUIDE BOOKS:	
START POINT:	DISTANCE:
ROUTE OUTLINE:	
WEATHER:	
COMMENTS:	
PUB:	
BIRDS:	FLOWERS:

WALK NO:	DATE:
COUNTY/AREA:	
MAPS USED:	
GUIDE BOOKS:	
START POINT:	DISTANCE:
ROUTE OUTLINE:	
WEATHER:	
COMMENTS:	
PUB:	
BIRDS:	FLOWERS:

WALK NO:	DATE:
COUNTY/AREA:	
MAPS USED:	
GUIDE BOOKS:	
START POINT:	DISTANCE:
ROUTE OUTLINE:	
WEATHER:	
COMMENTS:	
PUB:	
BIRDS:	FLOWERS:

WALK NO:	DATE:
COUNTY/AREA:	
MAPS USED:	
GUIDE BOOKS:	
START POINT:	DISTANCE:
ROUTE OUTLINE:	

WEATHER:

COMMENTS:

PUB:

BIRDS:	FLOWERS:

WALK NO:	DATE:
COUNTY/AREA:	
MAPS USED:	
GUIDE BOOKS:	
START POINT:	DISTANCE:
ROUTE OUTLINE:	
WEATHER:	
COMMENTS:	
PUB:	
BIRDS:	FLOWERS:

WALK NO:	DATE:
COUNTY/AREA:	
MAPS USED:	
GUIDE BOOKS:	
START POINT:	DISTANCE:
ROUTE OUTLINE:	
WEATHER:	
COMMENTS:	
PUB:	
BIRDS:	FLOWERS:

WALK NO:	DATE:
COUNTY/AREA:	
MAPS USED:	
GUIDE BOOKS:	
START POINT:	DISTANCE:
ROUTE OUTLINE:	
WEATHER:	
COMMENTS:	

PUB:

BIRDS:	FLOWERS:

WALK NO:	DATE:

COUNTY/AREA:

MAPS USED:

GUIDE BOOKS:

START POINT:	DISTANCE:

ROUTE OUTLINE:

WEATHER:

COMMENTS:

PUB:

BIRDS:	FLOWERS:

WALK NO:	DATE:
COUNTY/AREA:	
MAPS USED:	
GUIDE BOOKS:	
START POINT:	DISTANCE:
ROUTE OUTLINE:	
WEATHER:	
COMMENTS:	
PUB:	
BIRDS:	FLOWERS:

WALK NO:	DATE:
COUNTY/AREA:	
MAPS USED:	
GUIDE BOOKS:	
START POINT:	DISTANCE:
ROUTE OUTLINE:	
WEATHER:	
COMMENTS:	
PUB:	
BIRDS:	FLOWERS:

WALK NO:	DATE:
COUNTY/AREA:	
MAPS USED:	
GUIDE BOOKS:	
START POINT:	DISTANCE:
ROUTE OUTLINE:	
WEATHER:	
COMMENTS:	
PUB:	
BIRDS:	FLOWERS:

WALK NO:	DATE:
COUNTY/AREA:	
MAPS USED:	
GUIDE BOOKS:	
START POINT:	DISTANCE:
ROUTE OUTLINE:	
WEATHER:	
COMMENTS:	
PUB:	
BIRDS:	FLOWERS:

WALK NO:	DATE:
COUNTY/AREA:	
MAPS USED:	
GUIDE BOOKS:	
START POINT:	DISTANCE:
ROUTE OUTLINE:	
WEATHER:	
COMMENTS:	
PUB:	
BIRDS:	FLOWERS:

WALK NO:	DATE:
COUNTY/AREA:	
MAPS USED:	
GUIDE BOOKS:	
START POINT:	DISTANCE:
ROUTE OUTLINE:	
WEATHER:	
COMMENTS:	
PUB:	
BIRDS:	FLOWERS:

WALK NO:	DATE:
COUNTY/AREA:	
MAPS USED:	
GUIDE BOOKS:	
START POINT:	DISTANCE:
ROUTE OUTLINE:	
WEATHER:	
COMMENTS:	
PUB:	
BIRDS:	FLOWERS:

WALK NO:	DATE:
COUNTY/AREA:	
MAPS USED:	
GUIDE BOOKS:	
START POINT:	DISTANCE:
ROUTE OUTLINE:	
WEATHER:	
COMMENTS:	
PUB:	
BIRDS:	FLOWERS:

WALK NO:	DATE:
COUNTY/AREA:	
MAPS USED:	
GUIDE BOOKS:	
START POINT:	DISTANCE:
ROUTE OUTLINE:	
WEATHER:	
COMMENTS:	
PUB:	
BIRDS:	FLOWERS:

WALK NO:	DATE:
COUNTY/AREA:	
MAPS USED:	
GUIDE BOOKS:	
START POINT:	DISTANCE:
ROUTE OUTLINE:	
WEATHER:	
COMMENTS:	
PUB:	
BIRDS:	FLOWERS:

WALK NO:	DATE:
COUNTY/AREA:	
MAPS USED:	
GUIDE BOOKS:	
START POINT:	DISTANCE:
ROUTE OUTLINE:	
WEATHER:	
COMMENTS:	
PUB:	
BIRDS:	FLOWERS:

WALK NO:	DATE:
COUNTY/AREA:	
MAPS USED:	
GUIDE BOOKS:	
START POINT:	DISTANCE:
ROUTE OUTLINE:	
WEATHER:	
COMMENTS:	
PUB:	
BIRDS:	FLOWERS:

CHALLENGE WALK RECORD

WALK	DATE:
COUNTY/AREA:	
MAPS USED:	
GUIDE BOOKS:	
START POINT:	DISTANCE:
ROUTE OUTLINE:	
WEATHER:	
COMMENTS:	

PUB:

BIRDS:	FLOWERS:

WALK	DATE:
COUNTY/AREA:	
MAPS USED:	
GUIDE BOOKS:	
START POINT:	DISTANCE:
ROUTE OUTLINE:	
WEATHER:	
COMMENTS:	
PUB:	
BIRDS:	FLOWERS:

WALK	DATE:
COUNTY/AREA:	
MAPS USED:	
GUIDE BOOKS:	
START POINT:	DISTANCE:
ROUTE OUTLINE:	
WEATHER:	
COMMENTS:	
PUB:	
BIRDS:	FLOWERS:

WALK	DATE:
COUNTY/AREA:	
MAPS USED:	
GUIDE BOOKS:	
START POINT:	DISTANCE:
ROUTE OUTLINE:	
WEATHER:	
COMMENTS:	
PUB:	
BIRDS:	FLOWERS:

WALK	DATE:
COUNTY/AREA:	
MAPS USED:	
GUIDE BOOKS:	
START POINT:	DISTANCE:
ROUTE OUTLINE:	
WEATHER:	
COMMENTS:	
PUB:	
BIRDS:	FLOWERS:

WALK	DATE:
COUNTY/AREA:	
MAPS USED:	
GUIDE BOOKS:	
START POINT:	DISTANCE:
ROUTE OUTLINE:	
WEATHER:	
COMMENTS:	
PUB:	
BIRDS:	FLOWERS:

JOHN MERRILL CHALLENGE WALKS— devised, created and inaugurated by John N. Merrill.

DAY CHALLENGE WALKS

JOHN MERRILL'S
PEAK DISTRICT CHALLENGE WALK—25 MILES

Circular walk starting from Bakewell and involves 3,600 feet of ascent, while passing through typical Peak District scenery · river valleys, gritstone moorlands and outcrops, and limestone dales and plateaux. Interlaced are many historical items and eight inns! Whilst the walk is a challenge to walk in a day—about 10 hours—there is no time limit.

JOHN MERRILL'S
YORKSHIRE DALES CHALLENGE WALK—23 MILES

Circular walk starting from Kettlewell, in the heart of the Dales. The walk is a challenge to complete within twelve hours and involves 3,600 feet of ascent while encompassing the scenic variety to be found in the National Park— mountains, moorlands, limestone country and dale walking.

JOHN MERRILL'S
NORTH YORKSHIRE MOORS CHALLENGE WALK—24 MILES

A seaside bash! Circular walk from Goathland in the heart of the moors. The route combines moorland, river valley and coastal walking, using Robin Hood's Bay as the half-way point, and involves 2,000 feet of ascent.

PEAK DISTRICT END TO END WALKS—23 and 24 MILES

John Merrill's two favourite long walks in the Peak District—both he has walked more than thirty times! The Gritstone Edge Walk—23 miles, is downhill along the eastern edge system. The Limestone Dale Walk—24 miles, is down the limestone dales from Buxton to Ashbourne. Both are the grandslam of Peak District beauty.

THE LITTLE JOHN CHALLENGE WALK—28 MILES

Circular walk from Edwinstowe in Sherwood Forest, the heart of Robin Hood Country. Slightly longer day challenge but flat country passing through forest, meadering rivers, gorges and historical houses. A really superb walk!

MULTIPLE DAY CHALLENGE WALKS

THE RIVERS' WAY—43 MILES

The route crosses the Peak District from the start of the Pennine Way in Edale, to Ilam in the south. On the way you traverse the wealth of scenic splendour of the area and link the five principal rivers together—Noe, Derwent, Wye, Dove and Manifold. It is a challenge to walk it all in one day—about 14 hours—but is best walked in two or four days. There are numerous campsites, hostels and accomodation en route together with more than a dozen inns!

THE LIMEY WAY—40 MILES

John Merrill's classic walk down the limestone dales of the Peak District, starting from Castleton. The route takes you through twenty limestone dales to Dove Dale and Thorpe in the south. The walk is a challenge to complete within 24 hours—a red badge—or 48 hours—a green badge. Camp sites, hostels and more than ten inns lie along the route, while passing through stunning scenery.

THE PEAK DISTRICT—HIGH LEVEL ROUTE—90 MILES

Circular route from Matlock around the edge of the Peak District National Park. The route keeps to the highest and most rugged parts as it weaves it s way from Matlock across the limestone plateau to Dove Dale. Here it heads north to the Roaches and Shining Tor. The northern end traverses Chinley Churn before crossing the southern edge of Kinder to Ladybower Reservoir. The eastern side follows the whole Gritstone Edge system from Stanage to Beeley before descending to the river Derwent and back to Matlock. A hard six day walk with numerous inns, camp sites and accomodation along the way.

THE PEAKLAND WAY—100 MILES

John Merrill's classic circular walk around the Peak District, starting from Ashbourne. Broken down into eight easy stages this walk is ideal for a week's backpacking, walking or hostelling. The beauty of the walk lies in the variety of the scenery. Here in one fell swoop you see the scenic variety of limestone dales, gritstone moorland and edges. Interwoved are many historical buildings and fascinating legends—it is a walk for all.

PEAK DISTRICT MARATHONS

The first book to describe all the challenge walks in the Peak District area—more than 30 long distance routes. Some are challenge walks to be completed in a day; others require several days to complete. They range from 8 to 280 miles long—enough to satisfy anyone's appetite. All routes have basic maps, photographs and map and book lists together with principal information on the route and who to apply for badges.

ABOUT THE GUIDE BOOKS—

Each guide details the route with clear maps, text and photographs. The route is broken down into stages and an Amenities Guide details what accommodation and facilities are available en route. A log is provided to enable you to record your walk and a Trail Profile explains how much ascending and descending is required.

BADGES—

Four-colour embroidered cloth badges are available for each walk and are priced £1.75 each including VAT, postage, and a signed completion certificate by John N. Merrill. They are only sold to people who have walked the entire route and are only available from JNM Publications. The badges measure 75mm wide by 90mm high.

As many people have now walked more than one of his challenge walks or some twice, a special circular cloth badge—JOHN MERRILL WALK BADGE—is available priced £1.75. The badge measures 80m.m. in diameter.

RECORDS—

A master record of all known people who have walked a specific route is kept by John.

GUIDE BOOKS—

Are available direct from JNM Publications (autographed free) or from your local book store or outdoor centre.

J.N.M. PUBLICATIONS,
WINSTER,
MATLOCK,
DERBYSHIRE.
DE4 2DQ

JOHN MERRILL
CHALLENGE WALK BADGES

All badges are four colour embroidered on different coloured cloths and measure 2¾" wide by 3½" high. The special circular John Merrill Walk badge measures 3½" in diameter. The Limey Way and Peakland Way badges are 2½" in diameter with a walking boot as the logo. The walk badges for John Merrill's own walks are only available to people who have actually walked the whole route, and a signed completion certificate is issued. The Pennine Way badge is available to everyone. All badges cost £1.75, which includes signed certificate, VAT and postage.

BADGES AVAILABLE

JOHN MERRILL'S
PEAK DISTRICT CHALLENGE WALK

JOHN MERRILL'S
YORKSHIRE DALES CHALLENGE WALK

JOHN MERRILL'S
NORTH YORKSHIRE MOORS CHALLENGE WALK

THE LITTLE JOHN CHALLENGE

PEAK DISTRICT END TO END WALKS

THE RIVERS WAY

THE LIMEY WAY

PEAK DISTRICT: HIGH LEVEL ROUTE

THE PEAKLAND WAY

THE PENNINE WAY

JOHN MERRILL WALK BADGE

JOHN MERRILL CANAL WALK BADGE

ORDER FORM

NAME_____

ADDRESS_____

_____

I confirm that I have walked_____

_____

_____

Dates_____

Number of badges @ £1.75 each_____

Signed_____

SHERPA WITH LOAD—EVEREST BOUND

EQUIPMENT NOTES—some personal thoughts

BOOTS—preferably with a leather upper, of medium weight, with a vibram sole. I always add a foam cushioned insole to help cushion the base of my feet.

SOCKS—I generally wear two thick pairs as this helps to minimise blisters. The inner pair of loop stitch variety and approximately 80% wool. The outer a thick rib pair of approximately 80% wool.

WATERPROOFS—for general walking I wear a T shirt or shirt with a cotton wind jacket on top. You generate heat as you walk and I prefer to layer my clothes to avoid getting too hot. Depending on the season will dictate how many layers you wear. In soft rain I just use my wind jacket for I know it quickly dries out. In heavy downpours I slip on a neoprene lined cagoule, and although hot and clammy it does keep me reasonably dry. Only in extreme conditions will I don overtrousers, much preferring to get wet and feel comfortable.

FOOD—as I walk I carry bars of chocolate, for they provide instant energy and are light to carry. In winter a flask of hot coffee is welcome. I never carry water and find no hardship from doing so, but this is a personal matter. From experience I find the more I drink the more I want. You should always carry some extra food such as Kendal Mint Cake for emergencies.

RUCKSACK—for day walking I use a climbing rucksac of about 40 litre capacity and although excess space it does mean that the sac is well padded and with a shoulder strap. Inside apart from the basics for the day I carry gloves, balaclava, spare pullover and a pair of socks.

MAP & COMPASS—when I am walking I always have the relevant map—usually 1:25,000 scale—open in my hand. This enables me to constantly check that I am walking the right way. In case of bad weather I carry a Silva type compass, which once mastered gives you complete confidence in thick cloud or mist.

OTHER BOOKS BY JOHN N. MERRILL

WALKING IN DERBYSHIRE
MOTORING IN DERBYSHIRE
FAMOUS DERBYSHIRE HOMES
ASHBOURNE—A VISITOR'S GUIDE
BAKEWELL—A VISITOR'S GUIDE
MATLOCK—A VISITOR'S GUIDE
DERBYSHIRE FACTS AND RECORDS
DERBYSHIRE TRAILS
EXPLORE DERBYSHIRE BY CAR
EXPLORE THE PEAK DISTRICT
LEGENDS OF DERBYSHIRE
PEAK DISTRICT WALKS NO 1—SHORT WALKS FOR THE MOTORIST
PEAK DISTRICT WALKS NO 2—LONG WALKS FOR THE RAMBLER
THE LIMEY WAY
THE PEAK DISTRICT A TO Z
THE PEAKLAND WAY
WALKING IN SOUTH DERBYSHIRE
WALKS IN THE WHITE PEAK
WALKS IN THE DARK PEAK
JOHN MERRILL'S FAVOURITE WALKS
LOCKWOOD & CARLISLE LTD—A HUNDRED YEARS OF HISTORY
NO THROUGH ROAD—(MAJOR WRITER)
TURN RIGHT AT LAND'S END
FROM ARRAN TO ORKNEY
DISCOVER SOUTH YORKSHIRE
LEGENDS OF THE MIDLANDS
LEGENDS OF THE NORTH WEST
WALKING MY WAY
SHORT CIRCULAR WALKS IN THE PEAK DISTRICT
40 SHORT CIRCULAR WALKS IN THE PEAK DISTRICT
LONG CIRCULAR WALKS IN THE PEAK DISTRICT
CIRCULAR WALKS IN WESTERN PEAKLAND
CIRCULAR WALKS IN THE STAFFORDSHIRE MOORLANDS
PEAK DISTRICT TOWN WALKS
SHORT CIRCULAR WALKS IN THE DUKERIES
CANAL WALKS VOL 1—DERBYSHIRE & NOTTINGHAMSHIRE
HIKE TO BE FIT....STROLLING WITH JOHN
STRIDING WITH MERRILL
JOHN MERRILL'S PEAK DISTRICT CHALLENGE WALK
JOHN MERRILL'S YORKSHIRE DALES CHALLENGE WALK
JOHN MERRILL'S NORTH YORKSHIRE MOORS CHALLENGE WALK
PEAK DISTRICT END TO END WALKS
THE LITTLE JOHN CHALLENGE WALK
THE RIVERS' WAY
PEAK DISTRICT: HIGH LEVEL ROUTE
PEAK DISTRICT MARATHONS
DERBYSHIRE INNS
100 HALLS AND CASTLES OF THE PEAK DISTRICT & DERBYSHIRE

TOURING THE PEAK DISTRICT & DERBYSHIRE BY CAR
DERBYSHIRE FOLKLORE
LOST INDUSTRIES OF DERBYSHIRE
PUNISHMENT IN DERBYSHIRE
CUSTOMS OF THE PEAK DISTRICT & DERBYSHIRE
WINSTER—A VISITOR'S GUIDE
ARKWRIGHT OF CROMFORD
WITH MUSTARD ON MY BACK
EMERALD COAST WALK
TURN RIGHT AT DEATH VALLEY

OTHER BOOKS BY JOHN N.MERRILL & PUBLISHED BY JNM PUBLICATIONS

DAY WALK GUIDES

PEAK DISTRICT: SHORT CIRCULAR WALKS Fifteen carefully selected walks—3 to 5 miles—starting from a car park. The walks cover the variety of the area—the gritstone edges, limestone dales, and peat moorland. All follow well defined paths; include a pub for lunch; and are suitable for all the family. 44 pages 16 maps 32 photographs   ISBN 0 907496 16 4

PEAK DISTRICT TOWN WALKS Twelve short circular walks around the principal towns and villages of the Peak District. Including Castleton, Buxton, Hathersage, Eyam,Tissington and Ashbourne. Each walk has a detailed map and extensive historical notes complete with pictures. 60 pages 12 maps 96 photographs   ISBN 0 907496 20 2

PEAK DISTRICT: LONG CIRCULAR WALKS Fifteen differing walks 12 to 18 miles long for the serious hiker. Many follow lesser used paths in the popular areas, giving a different perspective to familiar landmarks. 64 pages 16 maps 28 photographs ISBN 0 907496 17 2

WESTERN PEAKLAND—CIRCULAR WALKS The first book to cover this remarkably attractive side of the National Park—west of Buxton. The guide combines both long and short walks. 25 -3 to 11 mile long walks with extremely detailed maps to help you explore the area. 48 pages 23 maps 22 photographs   ISBN 0 907496 15 6

12 SHORT CIRCULAR WALKS AROUND MATLOCK 12 walks of about 4 miles long into the Matlock area rich in history and folklore and make ideal family outings. Included is an 'alpine' walk, using Matlock Bath's cable car as part of the route. 52 pages 44 photographs 12 maps   ISBN 0 907496 25 3

SHORT CIRCULAR WALKS IN THE DUKERIES More than 25 walks in the Nottinghamshire/Sherwood Forest area, past many of the historic buildings that make up the Dukeries area.   ISBN 0 907496 29 6

DERBYSHIRE AND THE PEAK DISTRICT CANAL WALKS More than 20 walks both short and long along the canals in the area—Cromford, Erewash, Chesterfield, Derby, Trent, Peak Forest and Macclesfield canals.   ISBN 0 907496 30 X

66

HIKE TO BE FIT: STROLLING WITH JOHN John Merrill's personal guide to walking in the countryside to keep fit and healthy. He describes what equipment to use, where to go, how to map read, use a compass and what to do about blisters! 36 pages 23 photos 2 sketches 3 charts   ISBN 0 907496 19 9

CHALLENGE WALKS

JOHN MERRILL'S PEAK DISTRICT CHALLENGE WALK A 25 mile circular walk from Bakewell, across valleys and heights involving 3,700 feet of ascent. More than 2,000 people have already completed the walk. A badge and completion certificate is available to those who complete. 32 pages 18 photographs 9 maps   ISBN 0 907496 18 0

JOHN MERRILL'S YORKSHIRE DALES CHALLENGE WALK A 23 mile circular walk from Kettlewell in the heart of the Dales. The route combines mountain, moorlands, limestone country and dale walking with 3,600 feet of ascent. A badge and certificate is available to those who complete the route. 32 pages 16 photographs 8 maps   ISBN 0 907196 28 8

THE RIVER'S WAY A two day walk of 43 miles, down the length of the Peak District National Park. Inaugurated and created by John, the walk starts at Edale, the end of the Pennine Way, and ends at Ilam. Numerous hostels, campgrounds, B&B, and pubs lie on the route, as you follow the five main river systems of the Peak—Noe, Derwent, Wye, Dove, and Manifold. 52 pages 35 photographs 7 maps   ISBN 0 907496 08 3

PEAK DISTRICT: HIGH LEVEL ROUTE A hard 90 mile, weeks walk, around the Peak District, starting from Matlock. As the title implies the walk keeps to high ground while illustrating the dramatic landscape of the Peak District. The walk was inaugurated and created by John and is used by him for training for his major walks! 60 pages 31 photographs 13 maps   ISBN 0 907496 10 5

PEAK DISTRICT MARATHONS The first reference book to gather together all the major and classical long walks of the Peak District between 25 and 50 miles long. Many are challenge walks with badges and completion cards for those who complete. The longest walk—280 miles —inaugurated by John is around the entire Derbyshire boundary. Each walk has a general map, accommodation list, and details of what guides and maps are needed. 56 pages 20 photographs 20 maps   ISBN 0 907496 13 X

HISTORICAL GUIDES

WINSTER—A VISITOR'S GUIDE A detailed look at a former lead mining community which still retains a Morris dancing team and annual pancake races. A two mile walk brings you to many historical buildings including the 17th century Market House. Illustrated by old photographs. 20 pages 21 photographs 1 map   ISBN 0 907496 21 0

DERBYSHIRE INNS The first book to tell the story behind more than 150 inns in the Peak District and Derbyshire area. With details of legends, murders and historical anecdotes, the book gives added pleasure or impetus to explore the pubs of the region. Profusely illustrated with 65 photographs and a brief history of brewing in Derbyshire. 68 pages 57 photographs 5 maps   ISBN 0 907496 11 3

100 HALLS AND CASTLES OF THE PEAK DISTRICT AND DERBYSHIRE A visitor's guide to the principal historical buildings of the region. Many are open to the public and the guide describes the history of the building from the Domesday Book to the present time. The book is illustrated by 120 photographs and makes an excellent souvenir gift of one of England's finest architectural areas. 120 pages 116 photographs 4 maps
ISBN 0 907496 23 7

TOURING THE PEAK DISTRICT AND DERBYSHIRE Twenty circular routes of about 50 miles for the motorist or cyclist. Each route has a set theme, such as the gritstone edges or in the steps of Mary, Queen of Scots. Deatiled maps for each route and fifty photographs make this a useful companion to the Peak District/Derbyshire area. 76 pages 45 photographs 20 maps ISBN 0 907496 22 9

JOHN'S MARATHON WALKS

EMERALD COAST WALK The story of John's walk up the total length of the west coast of Ireland and exploration of more than fifty islands—1,600 miles. 132 pages 32 photographs 12 maps ISBN 0 907496 02 4

TURN RIGHT AT LAND'S END In 1978 John Merrill became the first person to walk the entire coastline of Britain—6,824 miles in ten months. The book details the route, how he ascended our three major mountains and how he found a wife. Included are more than 200 photographs he took on the walk, which is also a unique guide to our coastline. 246 pages 214 photographs 10 maps ISBN 0 907496 24 5

WITH MUSTARD ON MY BACK John has gathered together the stories of his first decade of walking—1970-1980. Here is a collection of unique walks in Britain, from a 2,000 mile walk linking the ten National Parks of England and Wales together to a 450 mile walk from Norwich to Durham. ISBN 0 907496 27 X

TURN RIGHT AT DEATH VALLEY During the summer of 1984, John walked coast to coast across America, a distance of 4,226 miles in 177 days. Few have walked across and none have taken so difficult a route. He crossed all the main mountain ranges, climbed 14,000 foot mountains, crossed deserts in 100 degrees, walked rim to rim of the Grand Canyon in 8 1/2 hours, and crossed the famed Death Valley. The walk is without parallel and the story is the remarkable tale of this unique adventure. ISBN 0 907496 26 1

STANTON, ON THE COTSWOLD WAY